TAMESIDE LIBRARIES

3 8016 0201 71528

KT-425-516

www. ⚡Tameside .gov.uk
HYDE LIBRARY
0161-342 4450

WITHDRAWN FROM
TAMESIDE LIBRARIES

THE SECRET LIVES OF INSECTS

...tines, Zombies & Jumping Beans

Extraordinary Insect Life Cycles

by Ruth Owen and Ross Piper

Ruby Tuesday Books

Published in 2018 by Ruby Tuesday Books Ltd.

Copyright © 2018 Ruby Tuesday Books Ltd.

All rights reserved. No part of this publication may be reproduced in whole or in part, stored in any retrieval system, or transmitted in any form or by any means, electronic, mechanical, photocopying, recording, or otherwise, without written permission from the publisher.

Editor: Mark J. Sachner
Designer: Emma Randall
Production: John Lingham

Photo credits: Alamy: 15 (top), 16 (bottom), 22 (bottom right), 26, 27 (top); Creative Commons: 8–9, 9 (bottom), 17; Dreamstime: 9 (top); FLPA: 6, 12 (top), 13 (top), 18–19, 22 (top); Getty Images: 25; Istock Photo: Cover; Macroscopic Solutions, LLC. www.macroscopicsolutions.com: 27 (bottom); Nature Picture Library: 7 (centre), 14 (left), 28; Ross Piper: 11 (bottom); S. D. Porter, USDA-ARS: 20–21; Science Photo Library: 24; Shutterstock: Cover, 1, 4–5, 7 (top), 7 (bottom), 8 (bottom), 10, 11(top), 12 (bottom), 14 (right), 15 (bottom), 16 (top), 22 (bottom left), 23, 29, 31.

British Library Cataloguing in Publication Data (CIP) is available for this title.

ISBN 978-1-78856-002-3

Printed in Poland by L&C Printing Group

www.rubytuesdaybooks.com.

Words shown in **bold** in the text are explained in the glossary.

Contents

Extraordinary Insect Life Cycles

Insects are tiny animals that have life cycles in three or four stages.

Almost all insects begin life as an egg. Some insects, such as cicadas and dragonflies, hatch from their eggs as a **nymph**. Insects such as wasps and butterflies hatch from their eggs as a **larva**, or caterpillar.

An emperor dragonfly nymph

A swallowtail butterfly caterpillar

Growing and Moulting

All insects have a tough outer covering called an **exoskeleton**. As a nymph or larva grows bigger, its exoskeleton becomes too small. The young insect sheds its old, tight shell. Underneath there is a new, larger exoskeleton. This process is called **moulting** and can take place several times as the insect grows.

As a nymph grows, its wings start to form. Finally, a nymph goes through its final moult and emerges as an adult.

Nymph exoskeleton

An adult dragonfly emerging from its nymph exoskeleton

What Is an Insect?

An insect has a body in three main parts — the head, **thorax** and **abdomen**. It has six legs and a pair of **antennae**. Most insects have wings.

Swallowtail pupa

When a larva is fully grown, it becomes a **pupa** and goes through a life stage called **pupation**. The adult insect emerges from the pupa.

Caterpillar exoskeleton

What Is Pupation?

Inside its exoskeleton, a larva's body undergoes huge changes to form the insect's adult body. Some insects pupate inside a protective **cocoon**. A larva might spin a cocoon using silk from its body. Other larvae build cocoons from soil or chewed-up wood.

Pupa case

A newly emerged swallowtail butterfly

Rumble in the Jungle

In the branches of a tree, in the steamy rainforest of Madagascar, there's going to be a fight!

The two competitors approach each other. The first to knock his opponent from the tree will be the winner.

The bizarre-looking insects are giraffe-necked weevils. During the mating season, males do battle by beating their long, giraffe-like necks together. And what does the victorious weevil win? He earns the right to mate with a female who waits close by, watching the fight.

A male giraffe-necked weevil

Giraffe-necked weevils only live on the island of Madagascar.

6

The Science Stuff

Once a male and female giraffe-necked weevil have mated, the female gets busy.

Female giraffe-necked weevil

The female weevil's neck is much shorter than the male's.

She uses her powerful legs to fold a leaf in half. Then she starts to roll up the end of the folded leaf.

Once she's made a tube-like leaf roll, she lays one tiny yellow egg inside the tube. Then she keeps rolling.

A leaf nest containing an egg

Finally, using her mouthparts, she strips the leaf from the tree. The rolled-up leaf nest falls to the forest floor. Then the female starts work on another leaf for another egg.

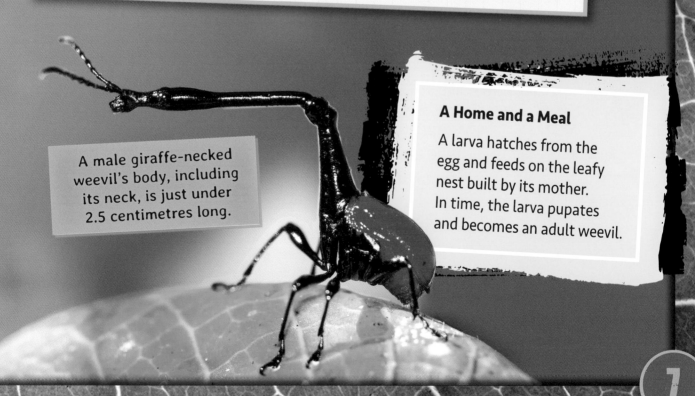

A male giraffe-necked weevil's body, including its neck, is just under 2.5 centimetres long.

A Home and a Meal

A larva hatches from the egg and feeds on the leafy nest built by its mother. In time, the larva pupates and becomes an adult weevil.

What Makes a Jumping Bean Jump?

You may have heard of Mexican jumping beans, but what exactly are they, and what do they have to do with the lives of insects?

A jumping bean is actually a nickname for a type of **seedpod.** These seedpods form on bushes that grow in the desert in Mexico. If a pod, or bean, gets warm, it may start to twitch and jump. Why?

The jumping bean is home to a tiny moth larva. When the larva feels its home warming up, it moves around inside the bean. This makes the bean twitch and roll away from the source of the heat. If the bean gets too hot, the larva inside will **dehydrate** and die.

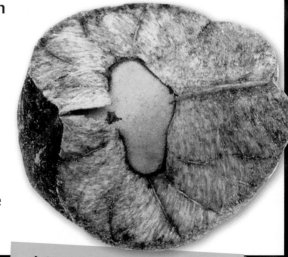

A Mexican jumping bean is about 1 centimetre long.

The Science Stuff
A Jumping Bean Moth's Life Cycle

① A female jumping bean moth lays her eggs on a jumping bean plant.

② A larva hatches from its egg and chews its way into a jumping bean, or seedpod. As the bean grows, the entrance hole seals up. The larva feeds on the inside of the bean.

Silk threads

A jumping bean moth larva

Jumping bean shell

A Bean on the Move

The larva spins silk threads from its body to the inside of the bean. To make the bean move, the larva twitches its body and pulls on the threads.

③ When the larva is ready to become a moth, it eats a circular hole in the seedpod's shell. Then it spins a cocoon made of silk around its body. Inside the cocoon, the larva pupates and becomes a moth.

④ The adult moth has no teeth to chew its way out of the hard bean, but that's not a problem. It climbs out of the pod through the tiny escape hatch that it chewed when it was still a larva.

An adult moth

A New Generation

Adult jumping bean moths only live for a few days. In that time they mate and leave behind a new **generation** of larvae.

9

Mummy's Going Hunting!

When it's time to raise a family, a female beewolf digs a **burrow**. She also goes hunting — for honeybees!

To make her burrow, the beewolf digs a tunnel in sandy soil. At the end of this main tunnel she digs shorter tunnels that lead to tiny rooms called brood cells. Inside each brood cell, the beewolf lays a single egg.

A female beewolf digging a burrow

A beewolf is a type of predatory wasp that hunts for bees.

Next, the mother beewolf catches honeybees and carries them back to the burrow. She places the bees in the brood cells. When her larvae hatch from their eggs, they have a meal of juicy honeybees waiting for them in their nurseries.

A burrow may contain about 1 metre of tiny tunnels.

Burrow entrance

A Very Fierce Mum

A female beewolf lurks around flowers. When a honeybee comes to gather nectar and pollen, she grabs it. The beewolf stings her **prey** and then carries it back to the burrow beneath her body.

Beewolf

Honeybee

The Science Stuff

A beewolf's sting **paralyzes** the bee, but does not kill it. A bee that is still alive will be fresher and juicier for the larvae to eat!

A beewolf places up to five bees in each brood cell.

Beewolf

Paralyzed honeybee

The mother beewolf licks the bees that she catches. She covers them with a special substance that stops them going mouldy.

Buried Baby Food

While beewolves hunt and bring food to their young, other insect parents take a very different approach. Their babies simply grow up alongside their food!

A pair of burying beetles finds the dead body of a bird, mouse or other small animal. The beetle pair then buries the **carcass** in the soil. Next, the beetles mate and the female lays up to 30 eggs close to the rotting body.

A burying beetle

Carcass

Finding Food

Antennae

Burying beetles have antennae that can detect chemicals being released by a dead body up to 8 kilometres away. If several beetles find the same carcass, they fight — male against male, and female against female. The biggest beetle pair usually wins the prize.

After a few days, larvae hatch from the eggs. The mother beetle feeds on the carcass and **regurgitates** a meaty soup into the mouths of her larvae. The larvae also eat meat from the carcass for themselves.

Mother beetle feeding a larva

Ball of meat

Larva

The Science Stuff

To prepare a dead body for their young, a beetle pair digs a hole beneath the carcass.

They strip the carcass of fur or feathers and then roll it into a ball.

Next they cover the ball with substances from their mouths and bottoms to stop it rotting too quickly.

Finally, they cover it with soil to keep it hidden from other insects.

A Beetle Larva Grows Up

After about a week, the larvae bury themselves in the soil to pupate. About a month later, they emerge from underground as adult beetles.

13

Beetles with Babysitters

Some insects actually let their neighbours provide food and a home for their young!

After mating, a female oil beetle digs down into the soil and lays her eggs. About two weeks later, tiny larvae hatch from the eggs. The larvae emerge from the soil and climb up a flower stem. Then they wait for a solitary bee to land on the flower.

Female oil beetle

Eggs

Some types of oil beetles lay more than 40,000 eggs.

The Science Stuff

What Is a Solitary Bee?

When you think of bees, you might think of honeybees or bumblebees that live in a hive. Solitary bees are bees that live alone and not in a large group.

A solitary bee

- Many types of solitary bees dig underground nests.

- There are almost 20,000 different **species** of solitary bees around the world.

Solitary bee

Oil beetle larva

Larva

When a bee visits the flower to collect nectar and pollen, the oil beetle larvae climb onto the bee. Then the larvae hitch a ride back to the bee's nest. Inside the nest, the larvae feed on the bee's eggs. They live in the nest until they are ready to change into adult beetles.

An adult oil beetle

Food Thieves

During their time in a bee's nest, oil beetle larvae also feed on pollen and nectar. This food was collected by the bee for her own larvae!

An Imposter Moves In

A large blue butterfly lays her eggs on a wild thyme plant. Then she flutters away, leaving the neighbours to care for her young.

After hatching and feeding on the thyme for a few days, the butterfly larvae, or caterpillars, fall to the ground. Next, the tiny caterpillars release chemicals from their bodies, called **pheromones**. The pheromones attract red ants. The chemicals fool the ants into thinking the caterpillars are ant larvae.

Large blue butterfly

Large blue butterfly caterpillar

The ants carry the **imposters** back to their nest. Once inside, the caterpillars have a juicy supply of food to feast on — ant eggs and larvae!

The Science Stuff

There are about 10 different species of large blue butterflies.

The caterpillars of some species feed on ant eggs and larvae.

Red Ant

Caterpillar

The large blue butterfly caterpillar in this picture is eating an ant larva.

Other types of large blue caterpillars fool their ant babysitters into feeding them. Worker ants bring the caterpillars **honeydew** and prey such as other insects.

Sometimes a caterpillar makes a sound like a young queen ant. The worker ants believe they are caring for a future queen. They feed the trickster first and give it more food than their own larvae!

Time to Leave Home

In time, a large blue caterpillar pupates and becomes a butterfly. Then the butterfly must crawl from the ant nest, leaving its tiny babysitters behind. Finally, outside the nest the butterfly can spread its wings and take flight.

A Zombie Cockroach

The way in which the emerald cockroach wasp raises her young is straight out of a horror movie!

When she's ready to lay an egg, the wasp finds a cockroach. She stings the much bigger insect to temporarily paralyze its front legs and stop it from defending itself and running away. Then, she injects chemicals into the cockroach's brain so it is zombified and unable to escape.

Zombified cockroach

Emerald cockroach wasp

The wasp leads her zombie prisoner into a small crack or crevice that will be her burrow. She lays a tiny egg on the cockroach's abdomen. Then she seals up the burrow with dirt and pebbles to keep out predators.

Zombie cockroach

Wasp egg

A larva hatches from the wasp's egg and begins to feed on the live cockroach. After about a week, the larva crawls inside its zombified **host**.

Powerless to escape, the cockroach can only wait for death as the larva feeds on its insides, growing bigger and bigger.

Wasp larva

What's for Dinner Today?

Scientists believe that the larva feeds on the cockroach's least important organs first. This keeps the cockroach alive for as long as possible. The larva needs its host to stay alive and fresh until it is ready to pupate.

When the cockroach finally dies, the wasp larva spins a silky cocoon and pupates. Finally, it emerges as an adult wasp and climbs from the dry, dead body of the cockroach!

Newly emerged wasp

Dead cockroach

Off with Its Head!

There's one very tiny fly that grows up inside an ant. In fact, to be precise, inside the **decapitated** head of an ant!

The female ant-decapitating fly lays her egg inside a fire ant's body. A larva hatches from the egg and crawls into the ant's head. Then the larva feeds on the ant's bodily fluids.

Female fly

Fire ant

Laying an Egg

The female fly stabs the fire ant with a body part called an **ovipositor**. Then she injects her tiny, torpedo-shaped egg into the ant with the ovipositor.

When it's time for the fly larva to pupate, it must be in a warm, damp place. The larva releases chemicals into the ant's brain that allow it to control its host. The larva directs the ant to leave its nest and family and crawl into some warm, damp leaf litter on the forest floor.

A decapitated fire ant's head

Ant's body

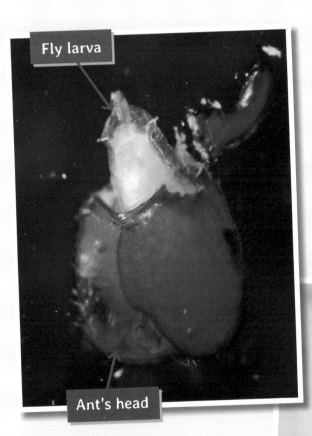

Fly larva

Ant's head

Now the story gets truly horrific. The larva releases chemicals into the ant that dissolve the **tissues** that connect the ant's head to its body. Eventually, the ant is killed as its head falls off. Then the larva eats the ant's brain.

A new fly emerging

Ant's head

Inside the ant's empty head, the larva pupates and becomes an adult fly. Finally, the tiny new fly crawls from the ant's mouth and begins its adult life.

Tongues, Stomachs, Intestines and Dung

When it comes to gruesome life cycles, insects don't only invade other insects.

A female horse bot fly lays her eggs on a horse's body. A tiny larva hatches from each egg and crawls up into the horse's mouth. Then the larva burrows into the horse's tongue or gums. The larva grows and moults, and after about one month, it crawls down into the horse's stomach.

A horse bot fly

Sneaky Invaders

A female bot fly may lay up to 1000 eggs on a horse. The eggs or larvae sometimes get inside a horse's mouth when the animal nibbles or licks the infested area.

Horse bot fly eggs

After about a year, the larva is ready to become a fly. It travels through the horse's **intestines** and when the horse poos, the larva leaves its host's body. Finally, inside the dung or in the soil, the larva pupates and becomes a fly. An adult bot fly only lives for a few days. It quickly finds a mate so it can reproduce.

Mammal Invaders

Bot flies use mammals as their hosts for reproducing. Different species of bot flies infest different mammals, including elephants, horses, reindeer, sheep and even humans!

Hooked mouthparts

A bot fly larva

The Science Stuff

The horse bot fly larva attaches itself to the horse's stomach with its hooked mouthparts.

It uses other mouthparts called mandibles to scrape tissue from the horse's stomach lining. During the year that it spends in the horse's stomach, the larva feeds on this tissue.

Flesh Invaders

A female chigoe flea gets ready to reproduce by burrowing into a person's skin — often on one of their feet. Then she starts to feed on her host's blood.

The flea's abdomen and rear end stick out of the person's skin, allowing male fleas to mate with her. After mating, the female's abdomen grows bigger and bigger as it fills with eggs.

Human flesh

Female chigoe flea abdomen

Rear end

Chigoe fleas are also known as sand fleas and jiggers.

After about two weeks, the flea releases up to 1000 eggs. Then the female flea dies. Larvae soon hatch from the eggs and live on the ground in sandy soil. After about a week, the larvae pupate and become adult fleas.

The Science Stuff

- A chigoe flea is just 1 millimetre long.

- As a female flea fills with eggs, she swells by almost 1000 times. Her abdomen may be bigger than a pea.

This illustration shows a female chigoe flea buried in skin.

Skin

Eggs

Swollen abdomen filled with eggs

The female flea breathes and poos through her rear end.

- Male fleas also jump onto hosts to feed on blood, but they don't burrow into the skin.

- Male chigoe fleas die after mating.

Dangerous Chigoe Fleas

Chigoe fleas can cause terrible pain and damage to a person's foot. The skin becomes inflamed and hardens around the flea, trapping the insect. Once the flea dies, its rotting body is still embedded in the host's foot, causing a serious infection.

Mini Parasites

Insects such as chigoe fleas and bot flies are parasites. A parasite spends all or part of its life living and feeding on another living thing.

Millions of Cicadas

The periodical cicada has one of the longest insect life cycles.

A periodical cicada nymph

When periodical cicadas hatch from their eggs, they are called nymphs. Some nymphs spend the first 13 years of their lives living underground in a forest. Others spend 17 years underground.

Periodical cicadas only live in the United States.

Adult periodical cicada

One night, when the time is right, each nymph emerges from underground at the same time as millions of other nymphs. The wingless nymphs climb up into the trees. Within an hour of emerging, their brown nymph exoskeletons crack open. Yellowish-white adult cicadas with wings squeeze from the nymph shells.

The Science Stuff

How do all the nymphs know to emerge at the same time? No one knows — yet. This is a mystery that future scientists still have to solve.

Nymph exoskeleton

Within 24 hours of emerging, the yellowish-white cicadas turn black and orange.

The cicadas fly in swarms through the forest finding mates. After mating, each female cicada lays up to 600 eggs in the trees. When mating is over, the cicadas die and their bodies fall to the forest floor.

Singing for a Mate

The noise in a forest grows louder and louder as male cicadas sing to attract females. A cicada's song sounds like tick, tick, tick buzzzzzz, tick, tick, tick buzzzzzzz.

Millions of tiny white nymphs hatch from the eggs. The nymphs fall from the trees and dig down into the soil. Under the ground, the nymphs will grow and change. Then, in either 13 years or 17 years, a new generation of cicadas will take flight!

This newly hatched nymph is smaller than a grain of rice.

Tiny Baby-making Machines

Aphids are tiny insects that are able to reproduce without mating!

In spring, aphid nymphs hatch from eggs that were laid in the autumn. Every one of the nymphs is female. The nymphs grow into adult wingless aphids that are able to give birth to more female nymphs. Soon, these new females are also ready to give birth!

Some of the aphids grow wings and fly off to live in new places. All summer, the number of wingless and winged female aphids grows and grows.

Finally, in the autumn, some male nymphs are born. These male aphids mate with females. Then the females lay eggs. In spring, the eggs will hatch, and the cycle begins again.

A rose aphid giving birth

No Males Required

When a female animal reproduces without a male, it is known as parthenogenesis (par-thuh-noh-JEN-uh-sis). Female aphids are able to reproduce both by parthenogenesis and by mating.

An aphid nymph

A Growing Family

A female aphid can be ready to have babies of her own when she's just a week old. She may live for about a month and give birth to five nymphs each day!

Wingless female aphids

Winged female aphids

There are more than 4000 different species of aphids.

The Science Stuff

Aphids feed on sugary plant juices. They suck up the juices through straw-like mouthparts.

Aphids produce a sweet, liquid waste product called honeydew. They squeeze the honeydew from their bottoms.

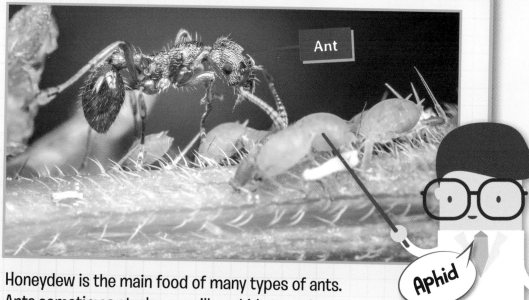

Ant

Honeydew is the main food of many types of ants. Ants sometimes stroke, or milk, aphids to make them release honeydew.

Aphid

abdomen
The rear section of an insect's body that contains its digestive system and reproductive organs.

antennae
Two long, thin body parts on the head of an insect that it uses for gathering information about its environment.

burrow
A hole or tunnel in the ground dug by an animal. Also, to burrow — the action of digging or burrowing into something.

carcass
A dead body.

cocoon
A protective case made by some insect larvae. A larva pupates inside its cocoon.

decapitate
To cut off a head.

dehydrate
To lose water.

exoskeleton
The hard covering that protects the body of an insect.

generation
A group of animals or people born around the same time.

honeydew
A sugary substance produced by some insects, such as aphids, as a waste product.

host
A living plant or animal from which a parasite gets its food.

imposter
A person or animal who pretends to be someone or something else.

intestines
A long tube inside an animal's body in which food is broken down.

larva
The young form of some animals, including insects, fish and frogs.

moulting
Shedding or casting off an outer covering.

nymph
The young form of some insects, between an egg and adult.

ovipositor
A tube-like body part on the abdomens of some female insects used for laying eggs.

paralyze
To make unable to move.

pheromone
A chemical released by an animal that affects the behaviour of other animals, usually of the same species. For example, an animal might release pheromones to attract a mate.

prey
An animal that is hunted by other animals for food.

pupa
A stage in the life cycle of some insects between being a larva and becoming an adult.

pupation
Changing from a larva to an adult insect.

regurgitate
To vomit up something that has been swallowed.

seedpod
A hard case that forms on a plant and contains the plant's seeds.

species
Different types of living things. The members of an animal species look alike and can produce young together.

thorax
The middle part of an insect's body between its head and abdomen. The thorax has six jointed legs and an insect's wings.

tissues
A group of connected cells in an animal's body that work together. For example, muscle tissue is made up of muscle cells.

Millions of Insects

Scientists have identified about one million different insect species. There are millions more yet to be discovered, identified and studied.

INDEX

LEARN MORE ONLINE

To learn more about insect life cycles, go to:
www.rubytuesdaybooks.com/insects